Memoirs of an Unsung Legend, Nemeso

Munyaradzi Mawere
&
Cosmas M. Mukombe
with
Christopher M. Mabeza

Langaa Research & Publishing CIG
Mankon, Bamenda

Publisher:
Langaa RPCIG
Langaa Research & Publishing Common Initiative Group
P.O. Box 902 Mankon
Bamenda
North West Region
Cameroon
Langaagrp@gmail.com
www.langaa-rpcig.net

Distributed in and outside N. America by African Books Collective
orders@africanbookscollective.com
www.africanbookcollective.com

ISBN: 9956-790-82-6

DISCLAIMER
All views expressed in this publication are those of the author and do
not necessarily reflect the views of Langaa RPCIG.

About the Authors

Munyaradzi Mawere is Associate Professor at *UniversidadePedagogica*, Mozambique. Before joining this University he was Lecturer at the University of Zimbabwe. Mawere is completing his PhD at the University of Cape Town, South Africa. He has written and published eight books and more than forty papers in scholarly journals.

Cosmas M. Mukombe was born in the Norumedzo area in Bikita in Zimbabwe and is one of the grandsons of Nemeso. He earned Builders' Instructors Diploma from the Institute of Penhalonga Technical College, Zimbabwe. Besides spending time building, Mukombe is a wonderful storyteller who enjoys reading. This is his first book.

Christopher M. Mabeza is a PhD researcher in the Department of Social Anthropology at the University of Cape Town, South Africa. At an environmental organization in Harare, Zimbabwe he spearheaded environmental education around the country. He has published on adaptation to climate by smallholder farmers in rural Zimbabwe and is researching water harvesting techniques in semi-arid southern Zimbabwe.

Dedication

For Cephas and Patrick

Table of Contents

Chapter One

Culture of the Duma

The Duma area was amply endowed with minerals and a rich cultural heritage. This is where Nemeso, a man with magical powers and four eyes, two in front and the other two at the back, was born. This area shared borders with Mandau to the east now known as Chipinge; the Rozvi and the Ndebele lived to the north, and to the south lived the Shangaans.

Many places in Duma were sacred. The place was inhabited by apparitions, and sounds would be heard resonating near the hills and rivers. Mermaids accounted for the disappearance of people near sources of water fountains, tributaries and big rivers. The sources of large rivers in the Duma area like Gande, Mujiche and Mukore were sacred, and ordinary people could not visit these places. At times, red, black and white blankets and various types of beads were seen at the sources of these rivers. Some said they saw river snakes at the sources of these rivers. Others testified that they saw lots of fish at these same sources. All these things were said to belong to the *Njuzu* or mermaids (half man half fish creatures) and therefore not to be touched. The greedy ones would try to harvest the fish, but the fish would disappear or turn into snakes.

Legend had it that mermaids did not like to be associated with dirt and that they lived in a paradise in the 'world beyond'. Thus it was not permissible to clean dirty clay pots or do any laundry at the sources of these rivers. Failure to observe these rules could result in sanctions like sand being thrown at perpetrators from invisible people. At times the perpetrators would run for dear life with a snake and at times a cow with three legs in hot pursuit. In rare circumstances the perpetrators would disappear only to reappear after many years as famed traditional healers. But those who had disappeared would only return on condition that the relatives of the victims do not mourn or say bad things about *Njuzu*, the mermaids. It is thought that the most senior mermaid would send its subordinates to spy on whether relatives of the victims were mourning or talking bad things about the mermaids. If relatives of the person who had disappeared mourned, then the victim would be killed by the mermaids and laid idle in a place where s/he would be easily seen by passers-by.

There were two other sacred places called Mapa and Marombo, where even angels feared to tread. Stones and trees in these places could not be tampered with. Rain petitioning ceremonies were held at Marombo. One of the prominent spirit mediums at the rain petitioning ceremonies was named Manyusa. Only elderly women would be allowed to brew traditional beer for the ceremonies. They also delivered the beer to Marombo and Mapa. Women who were still child bearers would not conceive if ever they went to these places – so only those women who had reached menopause or passed childbearing age would go.

Among all these places was a very important place under chief Bikita and headman Budzi. This is where Maringa Mountain is found. Long ago, on top of this mountain was a cave with a stone that could only be opened with the help of ancestral spirits. The cave was the burial place for the Duma chiefs as long as they had not usurped power or done immoral things. Therefore not all Duma chiefs were buried there. It took the intervention of the worldly-wise elders for the stone to open. Failure of the stone to open after these elders had pleaded with the ancestors was evidence enough to determine how democratic or moral upright a chief was.

The ill health and subsequent demise of a chief was a jealously guarded secret except for the chief's eldest son and the council of elders. When a chief's health deteriorated he was secretly taken to a cave not known by many people where herbs were administered on him by herbalists. The ailing and passing on of a chief was, as already alluded to, a secret and only the preserve of the chief's eldest son and chief ministers. In the cave, the chief would be attended to until he recovered or passed on. Herbs were administered by reputable herbalists and if the ailment was beyond their capacity they would summon an expert in foretelling the future and exorcizing evil spirits, normally known as a *n'anga* or traditional healer.

After the demise of the chief, the people would not be immediately informed. The elders would make a fire using traditional methods. They would use the fire together with herbs to mummify the chief's body.

After the mummification of the body, traditional singers, players of mbira, and elderly men and women were invited to the cave to play music. Meanwhile, the elders would be busy appealing to ancestral spirits to help open the stone covering the cave. If the deceased was well-liked by his people and morally upright in his deeds, then the cave would open. The elders and the traditional singers would then enter the cave still asking for guidance from ancestral spirits. At this time, the chief's body would be placed on a chair and the people present would then bid him farewell. Traditional singers would still be playing the mbira and the stone would close the cave. The elders would then summon the people who were the chief's subjects and living in the neighbouring chiefdoms and inform them about the chief's death. People would begin officially to mourn the chief until a new one was chosen. These were the traditional practices of the Duma before the advent of the whites and colonialism.

Besides respecting sacred places, the Duma people followed religiously many other traditional practices and respected prominent figures in their society. Among the prominent and highly regarded figures were *madzishe*/chiefs, *masvikiro*/spirit mediums and *n'anga*/traditional healers, *manyusa*/rain petitioners and *vauki*/diviners. These people were well regarded as the custodians of traditional practices and intercessors of the people, and this was long before white settlers arrived in the area.

The Duma people were expected to adhere to certain traditional practices. Transgression meant heavy sanctions, to deter would-be offenders. Witches and wizards had their ears cut for easy identification, and they would become the laughing stock of the Duma. The chief would order the offender's home to be destroyed, and the offender would be banished forever. Witches and wizards would not be welcomed anywhere and more often than not would become vagrants. Adulterers had their eyes plucked out and their reproductive organs removed. Thieves had their arms amputated and the veins of their legs cut.

Another traditional practice followed by the Duma was endogamy. The Duma believed in the moral conceptualization of rainfall variability, therefore, it meant that if you transgressed this practice then you would be held responsible for drought. Those who practiced endogamy were fined two head of cattle by the chief. Payment of these cattle meant you were no longer recognised as one of the VaDuma, and you went and lived on your own. Some of such offenders would when hearing about the demise of the chief, come back and forcibly take the chieftaincy. This meant that when eventually they died, the stone covering the cave where chiefs were buried would not open – a sign that their chieftainship was illegitimate and recognized by no ancestor of the royal family.

During those years, fruits, game, birds and rainfall were abundant because the Duma adhered to their traditional practices. They were also extraordinarily hard working. Duma became well-known, and its fame spread as far as the Ndau in the east and Ndebele in the west. People from Gutu as well as the Shangani and Ndau were involved in barter trade with the Duma. Spears, bows and arrows, hoes, axes, and domestic animals like cattle, sheep, goats and poultry were exchanged. The Duma grew in abundance cereal crops such as rapoko, millet, and sorghum, which they marketed. Those who did not have goods to exchange exchanged their labour for the grain. Poor families would exchange their young daughters for grain. The Ndebele, who had fled Chaka during the *Mfecane,* were said to mainly raid for grain, and this is said to have created bad blood between them and the Duma. The Ndebele during these years were known as the *Dzviti,* a derogatory name which suggested the discourteousness of the Ndebele people.

Men would gather around a fire outside where they discussed purely men's issues. Women lived in huts where they did chores typical for women like cooking and cleaning. Men constructed huts and did other chores like farming and hunting game such as rock rabbits, hares, and bucks. After a successful hunt, women would ululate and thank their men

5

for bringing meat home. Thanking as praise was done in the form of poetry and the man's totem. The skins of the animals were used as blankets and clothes. The animal skin used to cover the front part of the body was called *shashiko*, and the one covering the back part was called *nhahwamaringa*. Women were responsible for looking after their homes in the absence of their husbands. This was the nature of life in the Duma chiefdom.

Chapter Two

Growth of the Duma chiefdom

As time progressed young men and women began to marry. The elders began to practice polygamous marriages which led to an unprecedented growth of the Duma chiefdom.

The growth of the Duma also coincided with the rise in prominence of such chiefs as Pfupajena, Budzi also known as Bikita, Nhema, Masuka and Mutindi. The latter was father of Mukanganwi whose descendants still use the name Mukanganwi. These chiefs ruled under the name Duma although they had areas that came under their jurisdiction. As already alluded to, the Duma area stretched from Save to Runde. Near Save, the Duma area would share a boundary with the Ndaus' Chipinge ruled by chief Musikavanhu. To the north were the Rozvi under chief Jiri. Chief Neurungwe ruled the Hove in the far south. All these were friends of the Duma. This strong bond and rapport between the Duma and their surrounding chiefdoms lured the latter into a lull when thunderbolt struck in the form of famine never before witnessed. The Duma people were well-known as seasoned farmers who kept grain in their granaries for a rainy day. Maize, sorghum, millet, ground nuts, round nuts and rapoko were stored. Each type of grain was kept in its own granary. The Duma were so expert at preserving grain that some of the grain they stored such as millet could be preserved for as long as seven years. They preserved grain such as maize using traditional methods, for three to four years. Maize can be easily destroyed by weevils, but the Duma knew how to protect it from such predators.

The Duma had established themselves as the bread basket of the region. People flocked from near and far to buy grain from them. Some came from areas in the east under the jurisdiction of chiefs Mutema and Musikavanhu. Besides material things, some people brought their daughters in exchange for grain.

The famine thus brought lots of prosperity and women to the Duma, and this led to the growth of the population. There was food galore with the people spoilt for choice. The Duma also consumed the meat of domesticated animals obtained through barter trade. Transactions were through barter trade because there was no money. Chiefs sent their representatives to buy grain using silver and gold. The intensity of the famine led some chiefs to visit the Duma in person. One such chief was Musikavanhu who travelled to Duma with one of his wives and their young daughter.

Chapter Three

Musikavanhu's journey to the Duma

Early in the morning Chief Musikavanhu woke up his wife to begin the journey to Duma. The journey was long especially for women and children. He asked for guidance from his ancestors. His wife joined in as he did the necessary rituals in preparation for his journey. He started talking to his ancestors in a poetic and appealing manner:

Wabeta
Dhliwayo
Rufuramamberere
Majeketera
Majuru
Mazivanguva
Mauruka
Vachipanemwoyo
VaPfumairimumaoko
Vane musikana anenge ishwa
Mutukuti wangu yuyu
Vemhapachena
VaChibipitire
Vane runako runenge rweshwa
Inodyiwa nemanhenga ayo
Nyika yenyu ino yapinda rushambwa
Haichina rudekaro nerunyararo
Nhumbu dzavana dzava neminzwa inobaya-baya
Nyoka dzoraroguruguta munhumbu dzavana
Tarisai matenga akatsamwa

9

Akaramba kudonhedza yawo misodzi
Misodzi yedonhodzo nerupenyu
Ndirworwu rushambwa
Rwodai kusimudzawo neni nyana renyu
Muriritiriwo mhuri yenyu
Kuti timbonoshavawo kuvakazvipiwa namatenga
Sezvakareva imi
Chishiri chisingapambari hachinuni
Bva chiregai tinopambarawo
Pada tinganuna
Asizve honai nzira yacho mikwidza chete
Haina materu
Tingatoikunda chete kana matitungamirira
Mafamba nesu imi vedu
Tatorongedza kare
Chifambai nesu imi Mauruka,
Musatisiya tega Matsindira
Aiwa tatenda Wabeta
Tatenda!

His wife was reluctant to undertake the journey which was long and with potential dangers. However, she was motivated by the rituals performed by her husband and the fact that there was widespread famine. Chief Musikavanhu took his weapons which included an axe, a bow and arrows, and a spear. His wife carried their baby daughter, Mhepo, together with food provisions and water.

The journey was not for the fainthearted. The forest between Musikavanhu's area and Duma was infested with dangerous wild animals including elephants, hyenas, leopards, wild dogs and lions. Most of these animals used a drinking point on Save River which also served as a crossing point for people coming from Musikavanhu to Duma. This forest is the present day Save Valley Conservancy, an animal sanctuary.

After walking past an area known as Chipangai, the sun rose and the couple with their baby headed into the dense forest. They approached Save River which marked the boundary between Musikavanhu and Duma. As they journeyed, Musikavanhu and his wife encountered a troop of baboons moving from the south to the north. The troop crossed their path and melted into the dense forest. This sighting was symbolic of dangers that lay ahead, and Chief Musikavanhu and his wife pondered the perils. His wife broke the silence by intimating the potential dangers ahead. Long ago if a troop of baboons crossed your path, it symbolised potential trouble. You had to go back home and ask for guidance from your ancestral spirits or alternatively remain where you were and pray for protection from your ancestors and those of the forest. Any other silly move would mean danger or trouble.

The chief agreed with his wife that indeed they had seen the signs warning them of potential danger but said they could not turn back. Turning back meant death from famine. He suggested they ask for guidance again from their ancestors. The chief knelt and started appealing to his ancestors for guidance, now on a more serious note:

Ko nhai vakuru vangu
Wabeta
Dhliwayo
Rufura
Mamberere
Mauruka

VaChimapwere
Mutukuti wedanda
Majeketera
Majuru
Mazivanguva
Matsindira
Ko mati taresveizve?
Zvomogura nzira yedu iko kwatabva ruchingova rufuse?
Usiku utema
Gomo risina makwiriro
Zvino mati tiite ripi zano?
Tigare zvaramba
Tirare zvorwadza
Topeta maoko here tife zvedu takaringa?
Iyo mhuri yacho mati tiipei zvatangova misvuuganda?
Mati tava kutiza manyana nevhurenyu here?
Ko zvatakushumai wani chifambirwo?
Tiri kunoshava chete
Kuti tiwane kuraramisa iyoyi yamakatisiira mhuri
Tinodzoka kana tangowana chifambirwo
Saka kana ari mapfumo anga arodzva
Ngaafondodzwe
Kana iri miseve yanga yakungwa
Ngaidzoserwe pahwiriko
Kana zviri zvikara zvesango zvanga zvasosanzira
Ndosaka muriko imi munodyidzana nemhondoro
Varidzi vemasango
Chiombai chete dzose dzivatepasi
Nekwatinoenda ngazvive zvitambo
Tinozviziva kuti mwana washe murandakumwe
Asi ngatindogamuchirwawo sevanhu vane chiremera
Kana manga musinakunzwisisa

12

Ndinovimba ndazobaya dede nemumukanwa
Chiudzaiwo nevamwe vakuru venyu vose
Kuti nzira yedu
Ive tsvene isina mhingaidzo
Ngazvichiitwa tione Beta
Mauruka
Matsindira
Wabeta

After performing the rituals, the chief reassured his wife that danger had been averted and that they could continue tranquilly on their journey.

They immediately met people from Bvuma from chief Mutema's area. They were on their way from the Duma where they had gone a month before to ask for food. The people briefed Musikavanhu and his wife about the abundance of food in Duma as well as the dangers of travelling there. There was danger of being robbed when returning from Duma. The journey to and from Duma had become hazardous as hunger had changed the minds and traditional practices of many men.

When the chief and his wife were about to cross Save River, they saw a lion coming from the direction they were facing. The lion looked at them. The chief and his wife stood and looked back. The lion stared at Musikavanhu and his wife before it disappeared into the thicket of the forest. People were taught that when you came across a lion you were not supposed to run away from it but look it in the face. The lion is believed to be a very shy animal that cannot attack a person face to face and so would in most cases move away. If you ran from it, the lion would turn you into prey.

After crossing Save, the couple was relieved to see a group of people also travelling to Duma. These people were resting on a hill called Chishakwe. The place was teeming with game, and these people had apparently killed an animal and were feasting on it. Such was a God-sent opportunity for the chief and his wife to replenish their provisions.

The chief and his wife stayed with these people for a number of days before resuming their journey together. Before that, however, they ate a lot of meat and made a fire for roasting meat. They extracted salt near rivers where they would also kill small prey like buck. At night, they made a huge bonfire and slept around the fire so as to protect themselves from predators like lions and hyenas. During the day they hunted game and also dug the tree called Mutendeni which they dried and then ground into a fine powder for cooking *sadza* or thick porridge. The thick porridge they cooked was eaten together with game meat.

After about five days, Chief Musikavanhu and his wife continued their journey with the group of people they had just met to the land of VaDuma. They walked until they got to Chief Masuka's area, which was once under a famous chief named Jimu Rikonda. This area was close to Save Valley Conservancy and in between the latter and the VaDuma's territory.

Chapter Four

Mhepo's childhood

The widespread famine in chief Musikavanhu's area had led him to name his daughter, born to the wife with whom he travelled to Duma, Mhepo. Traditionally names carried a message. Famine, war, plagues of locusts and army worms, and other occurrences were understood to result from moral situations. Chief Musikavanhu thought that famine in his land was a result of his marriage to his relative of the beta totem. He thought this caused the rise of *mhepo* (wind) which troubled his land by striking it with hunger and famine. But it was too late. He thought to avail the situation because a child had already been born to the marriage.

Chief Musikavanhu slept for only one night at chief Masuka's court, bade him farewell and headed to the west to chief Pfupajena of the Duma people. Chief Pfupajena was very famous because of his farming skills, democratic rule and philanthropy. Musikavanhu had known Pfupajena's father during trading expeditions when the former was still a boy. Musikavanhu thought therefore that the only person who could help him was Pfupajenja. Musikavanhu's aim was to settle briefly among the Duma and go back during the rainy season that was to come. The anticipated generosity of Pfupajena and the threat of robbers and dangerous animals on his journey back influenced his plan to settle among the Duma.

Two days after leaving chief Masuka's court, Musikavanhu arrived at the court of chief Pfupajena. Many people, when they first saw him, were intimidated by his bulk and darkness. They thought him evil hearted, but their fears were allayed by his softspokenness. He spoke calmly and in a low tone except on very serious matters.

At Pfupajena's court, Musikavanhu and his wife were welcomed by Pfupajena's advisers. Musikavanhu told them where he had come from and the reasons for his coming. The advisers assured Musikavanhu his grievances would be brought to the attention of the chief in a few days' time. It was customary to announce a visit and the desire to arrange a meeting with the chief– bureaucratic and hierarchical process.

Chief Pfupajena was excited by the news of Musikavanhu's visit. Long ago it was an honour to be visited by another chief at your *dare* or court. This was thought to bring blessings or fortunes. However, it was rare for a chief to visit another chief. The standard practice was that when a chief wanted something from another chief, he would send his advisers. Musikavanhu was invited to meet chief Pfupajena at the royal fireplace.

"Your royal highness, it is my honour to be here at your court," said Musikavanhu.

"Welcome Beta!" retorted one of Pfupajena's advisers.

This was the first time for Musikavanhu to visit the present Pfupajena as chief, although some of the old advisers to Pfupajena knew Musikavanhu. Chief Musikavanhu was asked to brief chief Pfupajena on the purpose of his visit and after going through greeting formalities, he gave an account of how devastating the drought had been in his area. He explained that famine was widespread and that people no longer had anything to fall back on because of the drought. The purpose of his visit was therefore to ask for assistance in the form of food. Chief Pfupajena appeared to be touched by

16

the level of famine in Chief Musikavanhu's area. Some of the advisers of chief Pfupajena also appeared to be touched by this account. Pfupajena advised Musikavanhu that he would give him an answer the following day because he wanted to consult with his chief advisers. Musikavanhu was free to stay until he received the answer. This is what usually happened. The chief would not make a unilateral decision but had rather to engage in wide consultations before mapping the way forward. Some chiefs in those days, however, were individualistic and despotic and did not listen to their advisers.

Chief Musikavanhu lived peacefully and cooperated with his neighbours as compared to leaders like King Mzilikazi of the Ndebele people who in most cases was at loggerheads with him and wanting to raid his chiefdom. Pfupajena, thus, got the sympathy of Musikavanhu. And it was common for chiefs to cooperate in matters having to do with famine, war and marriage. When children were growing up they were told which families to marry into, and familiarity with the family was required. Children were instructed not to marry strangers as they would run the risk of marrying witches or murderers or persons with undesirable characteristics such as laziness. The saying: *"rooranai vematongo"* (marry your neighbours) was, therefore, very common.

Chief Pfupajena agreed to assist Musikavanhu with grain. It was also resolved that Musikavanhu would be assisted to carry the grain by some of Pfupajena's advisers given that the journey back to his chiefdom was hazardous. Musikavanhu was given the option of staying temporarily. Musikavanhu was very happy with this suggestion. He chose to remain in Pfupajena's area until the famine had ended in his own area. Pfupajena, through his most senior adviser, instructed the junior advisers to construct a shelter for Musikavanhu. The home was constructed at the foot of Mandara hill near the present day business centre named Makuvaza.

Chief Musikavanhu thanked Pfupajena for his generosity and hospitality. As time passed, Musikavanhu's daughter Mhepo grew. It turned out that she was both deaf and dumb. Musikavanhu engaged the services of traditional healers and diviners in the Pfupajena area to heal Mhepo but in vain. Even Pfupajena himself summoned some of the best healers and diviners in his land, but all efforts failed. Mhepo grew up to be a very beautiful girl. She was so beautiful that one would think she dropped from heaven. According to African folklore there is no woman who is perfect. A beautiful woman is likely to be either a witch or a thief. Mhepo was both deaf and dumb, perhaps as a compensation for her elegant beautifulness.

One day Mhepo disappeared from home. Her parents made frantic efforts to look for her but to no avail. Word of the disappearance of Mhepo got to Pfupajena who immediately launched a massive hunt for her. Every nook and cranny was searched but without success. The majority of the people thought Mhepo had been taken by mermaids. In the Shona culture if a person is said to have been taken by mermaids, the relatives should not grieve. After three days of a thorough search, it was decided to call off the search, and people returned to their homes and conveyed the message to the chief about their failure to locate Mhepo. The general belief that filled the minds of the majority of the people was that Mhepo had been taken by a mermaid to a world beyond the physical world.

On the fourth day, the most senior adviser of the chief summoned all the people for the purposes of enquiring if anyone had by then located Mhepo. The people were very sad, and fearful. They had failed to fulfil what the chief had ordered them to do. In those days it was obligatory to fulfil any chore ordered by the chief. During a war you could not flee from the enemy; instead you were to die fighting. Leaving the battlefront meant you could be labelled a coward and running away was punishable by death. When the chief's principal adviser stood up, people fell silent and were not sure about what would befall them, and especially the junior advisers. People suspected the chief's junior advisers would be punished severely for failing to find Mhepo. When the principal adviser to chief Pfupajena began to speak, a voice was heard saying, "Look I am now a mature girl."

Everyone looked in the direction of the voice and saw someone that looked like Mhepo. The principal adviser sent some of the chief's junior advisers to see for themselves and possibly bring Mhepo to the congregation. When they got to the scene, they saw it was indeed Mhepo standing on a dwala. They could not believe what they were seeing.Beside Mhepo was the king of the jungle, a huge male lion, and when the chief's advisers saw this, they wanted to run away but were stopped by a mysterious voice. The lion then disappeared, and Mhepo descended from the dwala to meet the people who had been sent. The people accompanied Mhepo who again could no longer speak. The incident was reported to the chief and people. The elders told the chief that the incident was symbolic and that the lion was not an ordinary one but could have been a *mhondoro*, an ancestral one. The hill where Mhepo had been seen standing was renamed Mhandara (a virgin girl) honouring the pronouncements Mhepo was heard uttering by everyone at the meeting.

Chapter Five

Mhepo's marriage and the birth of Nemeso

Back at her parents' home, Mhepo continued to grow physically, and her elegant beauty dazzled many potential suitors. The problem was how the young men would propose to her, as she was deaf and also stammered.

Chief Pfupajena's coronation after the death of his father took place before he had married or had a child. He married short thereafter at his young age, because it was believed that a wife helped in cementing the chief's rule. That explains the significance of the Shona proverb that a home is incomplete without a woman. Good leadership meant having a wife who would assist with many responsibilities including providing the chief with comfort and advice. Chief Pfupajena was attracted by Mhepo's beauty and hatched a plan to win her.

One day, the community organised a beer party to help weed the fields of chief Musikavanhu. Many people came to assist. Mhepo took her small hoe and went to weed in her mother's groundnuts field on her own. She often did this, as she appeared frustrated at seeing other people laughing at what she could neither hear nor respond to. Elderly women were sitting in the shade playing with children. Those days, old women were highly respected and could not be allowed to perform hard work like weeding. On occasions such as beer work parties, their duty was to play with the little ones. Meanwhile, others began seriously weeding chief Musikavanhu's fields. One could see only dust spiralling up into the sky. The elderly women sitting in the shade were ululating, and men were whistling. One of the elderly women was so impressed with the work that she ran to the fields and broke into a song titled *Vana kuhondo* (Send children to war).

Leader: *Gurayi hweeeiyewoye!*
Gurayi hweeeiyewoye!

Chorus: *Vanogarotumira vana kuhondo*
Hereiye kugarotumira vana kuhondo
Nhaka tinorima

L: *Gurayi hweeeiyewoye!*
Gurayi hweeeiyewoye!

C: *Vanogarotumira vana kuhondo*
Hereiye kugarotumira vana kuhondo
Nhaka tinorima

L: *Madzimai musaringa kuno*
Mukaringa kuno munoona pagere zvirombo
Zvisvikarudzi marovamwoyo
Shashiko nenhawamaringa zvazorora
Watarira tikuona nemborera paziso

C: *Vanogarotumira vana kugondo*
He he ha!
Vanotumira vana kuhondo nhaka munorima

As they continued weeding, people were inspired and motivated by the battle song – even though the theme seems quite serious to us these days. People would turn out in large numbers to partake in this ambiance at beer work parties.

Not only did they enjoy drinking, but also singing and dancing. Even chief Pfupajena on this occasion went about his business as an ordinary person. He took his hoe and joined others to weed the fields. After working for a while, Pfupajena saw Mhepo alone weeding in her mother's field. He pretended to be assessing Musikavanhu's fields and walked to where Mhepo was. Mhepo saw the chief coming and only smiled at him and continued with her work. The chief did not know what to say and started uprooting the groundnuts behind where Mhepo had weeded. On seeing this, Mhepo could not comprehend and started yelling at the chief. This attracted the attention of other villagers. Incidentally this was the first time Mhepo started to speak. The elderly women ululated, and others also showed a lot of joy with this development. It was clear to everyone that this occurrence was symbolic in the sense that the chief's and Mhepo's ancestral spirits had agreed there be a union between the two. There was no doubt, as previously traditional healers and diviners had been summoned to deal with Mhepo's problem but to no avail.

Efforts were immediately underway to take Mhepo to chief Musikavanhu as his wife. Mhepo was taken to the chief's home to be his wife. Pfupajena meanwhile arranged to pay the bridewealth to his in-laws including a herd of cattle. People approved of this union since Chief Pfupajena had helped Mhepo to talk, and besides he had been so generous to Mhepo's parents. The fact that Pfupajena assisted Mhepo to talk when even famous traditional healers and diviners had failed helped consolidate his fame and respect among his people and beyond.

After her marriage, Mhepo fell pregnant. Meanwhile Mhepo's parents decided to bid farewell to chief Pfupajena and go back to Chipinge, their homeland. Rains had been falling everywhere ensuring good harvests, and famine would be a thing of the past. On hearing about Musikavanhu's intentions to leave, Pfupajena provided the chief and his wife with people who would accompany them. Chief Musikavanhu was given a hero's welcome by his people who prepared a feast. The people who had accompanied chief Musikavanhu were very impressed, and when they went back they briefed chief Pfupajena and his wife Mhepo about their trip.

For the time being, Mhepo's pregnancy progressed well. Midwives were in attendance as the time of her delivery edged closer and closer. There were of course no hospitals as we know them today. A midwife was given a cow for her work of assisting a woman to deliver. This is because the work of a midwife could be risky and required illustrious expertise.

Mhepo's time to deliver finally arrived. It was on a clear moonlit night. After dinner, Mhepo started feeling odd. The midwives had already gathered twigs and pods of the *nhengeni* tree seed. The *nhengeni* seeds were used to give light as the seeds are fatty and with the capacity to produce a lot of light energy. From the time people had dinner, not many slept except for men who appeared not concerned about the process of women giving birth. At around midnight, Mhepo went into labour. The midwives did everything in their power to ensure a safe delivery of the baby.

The midwives were puzzled however by the appearance of the baby. The baby had four eyes, two at the back and two in front. The midwives were not sure whether they should kill the baby as was common practice when a deformed baby was born. Some of them contemplated strangling the baby but were afraid of the avenging spirit. Such a disability was the first of its kind in chief Pfupajena's territory, and even beyond. The midwives argued among themselves about whether they should ululate or not. According to Duma tradition, whenever a baby was born normally and alive, the midwives were required to ululate as a sign that new life had been given. Eventually they agreed for a subdued ululation.

There was no plan by sunrise regarding what to do with the baby. The midwives were not happy, because they knew what to expect from the chief when he would eventually hear the news of the deformed baby. Long ago if a baby was born deformed or a twin, it was interpreted as a curse. Midwives were urged to kill such babies. If the chief got wind of the occurrence, he would order that the babies/baby be killed. It was a tough task for the midwives to kill such babies, and it was equally difficulty to convey such a message to the father and worse still to chief Pfupajena. The midwives therefore took their time strategising before telling the chief.

Chapter Six

Mhepo escapes with Nemeso

The chief had heard subdued ululation while in his bedroom. He also realised on the following day that the midwives sounded like they were not excited. Besides, he had not been informed about the birth. All these things puzzled him, and he began to suspect there could have been problems with the delivery of the baby.

Chief Pfupajena became very curious and a little worried about what exactly was happening and decided to visit his uncle Mutindi. The other idea was to ask for advice about what course of action to take regarding the secrecy of the birth. Mutindi was the young brother of chief Pfupajena's father. He ruled the area to the north of Pfupajena's area, known today as Mukanganwi. Pfupajena was the eldest son and therefore the heir-apparent. When his father passed on, Pfupajena was still very young and sought advice from his uncle Matindi about how to rule his people. Pfupajena's father had enjoyed cordial relations with his young brother Mutindi. Moreover, Mutindi's home was not very far from Pfupajena as their chiefdoms were just side by side.

After consulting Mutindi, Pfupajena bade him farewell. Mutindi promised to come to Pfupajena's place at midday. After bathing at a pool near Mhandara, Mutindi decided to go to the birthplace of the baby. He greeted the midwives and enquired about the newly born baby. The midwives' answer suggested that all was not well. The senior midwife disclosed to Mutindi that Mhepo had given birth to a deformed baby with four eyes, two in front and two at the back.

Mutindi rose up and on his way to Pfupajena's home staggered like a rhino fed on stems of the *mukonde* plant. He was no longer of sound mind because of the news he had heard about the deformed baby. He entered Pfupajena's bedroom and took a deep breath. Pfupajena immediately suspected that something bad had happened. Pfupajena greeted his uncle as tradition dictates. Mutindi immediately broke the sad news to the chief. He said something strange had happened. He disclosed that Mhepo had given birth to a son with four eyes, two at the back and two in front. The two discussed what this could mean and the kind of action to be taken, with Pfupajena suggesting that Nemeso was supposed to be killed. A decision was reached that the chief would send some of his warriors to kill the baby, and Mutindi bade him farewell.

Mutindi began to think about the baby and Nemeso's future. He recalled that when he was growing up, it was normal practice for a midwife to kill a deformed baby immediately after it had been borne. By then however it was about three days after the birth of Nemeso. The fact that Nemeso had not been killed soon after his birth puzzled Mutindi. He sat on a rock as he pondered the next course of action, because killing Nemeso could lead to many deaths in the family because of the avenging spirit. At the same time, not killing Nemeso was also opposed to the Duma people's tradition. This situation put Mutindi in a great dilemma, and he was unsure of how to solve it.

He immediately fell asleep and dreamt about a lion with a shiny skin coming towards him. In the dream, Mutindi was very frightened because he had no spear or axe to fight the lion. As the lion drew nearer, it immediately changed into an old man with grey hair holding a walking stick. The old man started talking. The "voice" instructed Mutindi to help Mhepo escape with the baby to the far-east mountains called Mambiru. Mhepo should hide in the biggest cave in those mountains. Mutindi was instructed to help in feeding the mother and the baby. He was assured that no harm would befall him or the baby. Further, Mutindi was instructed not to disclose this information to anyone including his wife and his beloved Pfupajena. He was asked to immediately go and inform Mhepo about this message. Mutindi then woke up from his dream.

Mutindi sat for a while digesting his dream and contemplating whether to resist the dream or not. He soon realised that the lion that had appeared in his dream was an ancestral one. He also realised that the ancestral spirits did not want Nemeso to be killed regardless of what tradition dictated. Mutindi rose up and went to the hut were Nemeso and Mhepo were. The sky was a clear, and the moon was shining. He knocked on the door, and the senior midwife woke to make a fire while the others opened the door for Mutindi. Mutindi then requested an audience with Mhepo.

Mutindi disclosed to Mhepo that her son was going to be killed the following day, so she had to escape that night and go to the mountain as directed by the ancestral spirits. He assured her that she was going to be safe and that he would supply her with food and all other necessities within his power. Mhepo agreed to the plan, and Mutindi bade farewell to all and went back to his home.

Normally people fall into a deep sleep towards dawn. In the hut where the midwives were, the fire was almost gone with lots of ash having accumulated. The midwives were asleep and snoring. Rats were running all over the place as if they were holding a meeting. Mhepo woke up to begin to prepare for her escape. She covered her baby in a skin and took a pocket of maize meal and some other provisions for use in her new life and disappeared into the night as she began her journey to the mountains as directed by Mutindi in his dream.

Mhepo walked a long distance. Instead of getting tired, she felt like she was gaining in energy. She was comforted by the fact that she had escaped with her son from the jaws of death. She dearly loved her son despite the general perception by the people that he was a curse from the ancestors and God. She did not fear the predators in the dense forest. She was also comforted by the reassurance of Mutindi that she should not be afraid because the ancestral spirits would look after her. By midday she was getting closer to the mountain. At sunset, Mhepo arrived at the foot of the mountain which was later named Rumedzo. It was here that the boy was named Nemeso by the mother and Mutindi because he had not been given a name soon after birth. According to the Duma tradition, a child was not given a name on the very day of his or her birth. A traditional ceremony of naming a child was to be held a few days following the birth of the child.

She went up the mountain using a trail used by baboons until she got to the cave where she had been told by Mutindi to reside. When she got to the cave she gathered firewood but made sure not to enter the cave before doing some rituals. She prayed to the ancestors for protection while holding her baby.

Tasvikawo mugomo renyu rino Moyo
Chirandu, mushayachirashwa
Tinofamba nejeche renyu iri
Kutiza neupenyu

Tarisai kwatabva
Marimi emoto chete
Kwatinoendazve usiku
Chitivhumbamirai Chirandu
Murege kutityisa aiwa
Nemi vokwangu Beta, Dhliwayo
Rufura
Mamberere
Mutukuti wedanda
Diutiu
Matsindira
Majuru
Musikana anenge ishwa
Mune runako runenge rwesha
Vemhapa machena
VaChibipitire
Madzivire
Onai todzungaira namasango
Kuri kutsvaka kuraramisa irori nyana ramakatipa
Ngatichigarisika
Parege kuwana chinotivinga
Tarisai kana chouviri hatina
Tinovimba nemi sokuti ndimi vakuru vedu
Tinotya kana tiri toga
Chigarai nesu muno umu
Kusvika musi uyo tichazokuyenekai
Toendazve uko muchatiratidza
Ndatenda Mauruka, Dzikarinda
Aiwa zvaonekwa Beta
Matsindira

After asking for protection, Mhepo made a fire and entered the cave. The fire lit the whole cave. She had learned from chief Pfupajena that fire scares away wild animals including the most fearsome like hyenas, lions and leopards.

Chapter Seven

Mutindi's creative genius

When Mhepo disappeared from Chief Pfupajena's court, the midwives were accused of facilitating the disappearance. They were only spared from severe sanctioning because the most senior midwife was Chief Pfupajena's grandmother who according to custom was one of the few people highly regarded by the chief.

A manhunt for Mhepo and her son was immediately launched. Given that he was considered a curse to the whole Duma chiefdom,Mhepo's son was clearly on the death roll. The story of Mhepo and her son's disappearance spread like fire on a dry prairie. Pfupajena's advisers were summoned and sent to search for Mhepo and her son. Some were sent to Musikavanhu to find out if Mhepo had not escaped to her parents' home, but all was in vain. She was nowhere to be found. Word had also spread about the birth of Mhepo's deformed baby. Some joined the search for Mhepo and her son out of curiosity to see the first baby of its kind – a baby with four eyes. Others were baying for the blood of both Mhepo and her son. How could someone protect the life of a curse on the land?

After several days of searching for Mhepo and her son, the chief came to the conclusion that they might have been eaten by predators when they fled his chiefdom. Some thought that Mhepo and her son had been destroyed by ancestral spirits who were angry with both. Many theories, thus, were advanced about the disappearance of Mhepo and her son, but nobody really knew what had happened to the two.

Mutindi kept a very cool head and watched people searching everywhere for Mhepo and her son but did not disclose to anyone what had actually happened. He, like anyone close to Pfupajena, masqueraded as someone greatly troubled at heart by Mhepo's action. He recalled his dream. It was time to act because it had been a while since his daughter-in-law had hidden in the cave. Early one morning he woke up and sharpened his axe and spear and took his bow and arrows. He took some oil and maize meal. He told his senior wife he was going to Nhema's area in the west, the area called Zaka today, to scout for virgin land for growing crops. Mutindi promised to come back after three days.

Mutindi first went towards the west and then turned to the east where Mhepo had escaped. He walked slowly because he was now old but became more energized as his journey progressed. By sunset he was approaching Rumedzo mountain. He climbed the mountain and settled at an open space and gathered firewood for making a bonfire to scare away animals. Mutindi also thought of looking for a vantage point where he could spot where there was fire, and then he would know that would be the place where Mhepo was, as the mountain was surrounded by uninhabited forests. After a while, he heard a sound and saw an animal and shot it with his bow and arrow. He tried to trail it but it was already dark. He could hardly see, and so he gave up. Mutindi then followed a trail used by baboons and after walking for a short distance, he saw a fire. At first he thought the fire had been made by hunters who might be exploring the fortunes of the forests.

When he arrived at the place where there was fire, Mutindi discovered Mhepo busy breastfeeding her son. He stepped on dry leaves, and this alerted Mhepo of his approach. Mhepo was filled with happiness when she saw her father-in-law. She wanted to leap and hug him, but traditionally it was taboo for a daughter-in-law to make contact with her father-in-law. Mutindi undertook greeting rituals before going into the cave.

'Ehe-e tasvikawo kwenyu kuno
Moyo chirandu chegono
Mushayachirashwa
Mukaka tinomwa
Mafuta tichizora
Nyama tinodya
Dowo tichikakisa ngoma
Ndove tinodzurisa
Muswe tichifumhisa
Nyanga tichiita gonamombe
Vari Dikitikiti
Nevari Ushava
Mambiru
Tinotenda ndimi matitungamirira
Makatungamirazve muroora nejecherenyu
Ndivava vatadai kufambira
Kuti tivamutsire nokuona kana muchivariritira
Ehe-e tazviona munavo
Namangwana musanyara
Ngazvirambe zvakadaro gono redu
Musatisiya toga tinotya'

Ndatenda Chirandu
Zvaonekwa Moyo
Zvaonekwa Gono!

After the greeting rituals, when Mutindi entered the cave, he sat on a rock. His daughter-in-law knelt and greeted him. He gave Mhepo the parcel he had brought, and she was very appreciative. Mhepo realised that Mutindi was very principled because he had fulfilled what he had promised. Mhepo had not believed that her father-in-law would visit her, even though love for her son and belief in ancestral spirits had caused her to believe Mutindi's words about escaping with the child.

Mutindi added more firewood to the bonfire, and the whole cave was lit. He then asked for permission to hold the baby. He was pleasantly surprised that the baby had grown much bigger than the last time he had seen him. He asked his daughter-in-law the name she had given the baby. Mhepo replied that she had not given the baby a name. She added that she was of the opinion that Mutindi should give the baby a name as Mutindi was of the same blood as the baby. Knowing their tradition, Mutindi did not resist his daughter-in-law's words. He gave the baby the name Nemeso because he was the first baby in the Duma clan to be born with four eyes. Mhepo immediately ululated as a ritual to mark the occasion of the naming of her son. After holding discussion with his daughter-in-law, Mutindi made a huge fire and slept.

On the following day, Mutindi woke up early to trail the animal he had shot with his bow and arrow the previous night. Traditionally, hunters did not disclose their movements, and so Mutindi informed Mhepo that he was looking for a source of water in the surrounding areas

36

because water was becoming scarce in the wetland where Mhepo used to fetch it. Mutindi followed the trail of the animal he had shot. When he saw a trail of blood, he suspected it might lead him to the animal. He followed the trail then suddenly saw the dead animal beside a rock with the arrow still stuck in its body. Mutindi thanked his ancestors and continued walking on the trail eager to see how far it went. After walking for a short distance he saw a spring of water and immediately named it *Tsime raNemeso* or Nemeso's Spring, a name still in use today.

Just below the spring was a stream which flowed down the mountain. The spring was the source of the stream. He named the stream, Gande meaning it was a stream with water which is thrown. Mutindi walked farther and heard the noise of splashing water. The sun was about to rise. Mutindi was frightened, because he thought the noise was emanating from mermaids but decided to continue and investigate the source of the noise anyway. As he walked farther, the noise drew nearer and he continued walking under cover of the trees fearing that the mermaids might catch his sight. When he was closer to the source of the noise, he looked timidly and realised the noise was being made by water falling down some rocks. When he got to the scene, he thought he would see people playing drums. He enjoyed watching this natural phenomenon, the first of its kind he had so far witnessed since birth. He named the falls Chingoma, a name still used today.

Mutindi then returned to collect the animal he had shot. He took his knife and began to dress the animal. He carried the meat to the cave where Mhepo was and asked her to follow him so as to go and collect some more meat which had been left behind. Mhepo was very happy with the hunting prowess of her father-in-law. She thanked him by means of a poem for hunters.

Titambire Moyo, Chirandu
Titambire vahombarume
Mune uhombarume husina vazhinji
E-e! Zvaitwa VaMurondatsimba
Jengeta macheche
VaChireranherera vangu
Vari Dikitiki
Vari Ushava
Mushenjere waVaDuma
Usina pakaminama
Pakaminama munosabvura
Tichiita maonerapamwe
Chuma chomuzukuru
Zvaonekwa VaDzimba
Aiwa zvaitwa Moyo
Zvaonekwa Chirandu

Mhepo then joined her father-in-law to go and carry some of the meat he had left behind. Mutindi also showed Mhepo the spring he had named *Tsime raNemeso,* and this made Mhepo happy. The two carried the meat to the cave and cut it into smaller pieces before drying it on the fire as a way of preserving the meat. Each time Mutindi wanted to kill an animal, he would ambush it at Nemeso's spring because it was the source of water for most of the animals in the area.

Chapter Eight

Mhepo flees with Nemeso

Mutindi did not disclose to anyone where Mhepo and Nemeso were hiding. He continued to visit Mhepo and her son and help with provisions. With time, people began to smell a rat. His favourite wife began to suspect that something was amiss. When a woman wants something from her husband, she does all sorts of things to impress him. Ultimately a husband gives in and lets the cat out of the bag. This is what Manditserera, Mutindi's favourite wife, did when she wanted to know where her husband was going each time he disappeared.

One morning Manditserera prepared her husband *sadza* served with mice as this was Mutindi's favourite relish. The mice had been dried and were therefore easy to prepare. She put the dried mice in a pot and warmed them. She added peanut butter and pepper. After preparing the relish, Manditserera began to prepare a thick porridge using millet mealie-meal. She prepared it in a manner liked by her husband. She served her husband the food she had prepared. Mutindi could not help but salivate at the appetizing meal his wife had prepared. Manditserera's unlimited repertoire of cooking skills had won her a place as Mutindi's favourite wife. Manditserera then brought "milk" to her husband. At the same time, Manditserera was pouring beer in a mug for the enjoyment of her husband. Mutindi drank all the beer. Manditserera joined her husband and drank beer together with him. Because she was on a mission, however, she did not drink much beer. She continued to engage her husband in conversation at the same time assessing how drunk he was.

When she realised he was drunk, she began to flatter him. She asked him whether she was not doing enough to make him happy. Mutindi told her that she was the one he loved most among his wives. Manditserera then shot back and said that if he really loved her then he should tell her the place he was frequenting those days. Mutindi assured her that he loved her so much but did not disclose to her the place because women could not hold secrets. Mutindi was cornered and agreed to let the cat out of the bag on condition that Manditserera kept it a jealously guarded secret. Mutindi disclosed how he had assisted Mhepo and her son escape and how he regularly visited them and supplied them with food. Manditserera promised to safeguard the secret.

Mutindi continued to visit Mhepo and her son. He would not tell anyone where he was going except for Manditserera. One day Manditserera disclosed the secret to her best friend, Guhwa. Guhwa was a slim, tall woman. She was a chatterbox. The moment she started talking she would not stop. If she lived these days she would be nicknamed the Zimbabwe Broadcasting Cooperation (ZBC). Anyone who had missed out on the latest gossip would visit Guhwa for a briefing. Guhwa enjoyed cordial relationships with many people including Manditserera. Those who had something to hide never liked Guhwa, for she would expose them. Guhwa, true to her nickname, disclosed to all and sundry the whereabouts of Mhepo and her son, Nemeso. Within a short period, word had spread and got to the ears of Pfupajena.

When Pfupajena heard that Mhepo was hiding and that Nemeso was still alive, he was greatly troubled. What bothered him more was that his uncle Mutindi assisted

40

Mhepo to escape with her son. Mutindi was Pfupajena's special adviser, and so this made it difficult for Pfupajena to summon his uncle and ask him about the issue. What he could manage was to summon his other advisers and ponder the issue. Pfupajena and his advisers agreed not to ask Mutindi about this issue but to keep him under surveillance. This idea was conceived so that each time Mutindi would visit Mhepo's hideout, some of Pfupajena's advisers could track him until they got to where Mhepo and her son were and then send an army to kill them.

After Pfupajena and his advisers met, it was revealed to Mutindi in a dream. In the dream Mutindi saw that same lion which had been in the dream when Nemeso was born. The lion revealed to Mutindi that Pfupajena was planning to send an army to kill Mhepo and her son, and therefore Mutindi was not supposed to visit his daughter-in-law until the lion came back in a dream to instruct him to do so.

After Mutindi had this dream, he stopped visiting Mhepo and her son. Days passed, and Mutindi was nowhere to be seen. Mhepo's supplies of meat and mealie-meal began to be depleted. She thought Mutindi had fallen ill and therefore could no longer walk. Mhepo hatched a plan of digging a *mutendeni* tuber and drying it and then have it ground into mealie-meal. She harvested vegetables where there were animal droppings. The vegetables would grow big because of the manure of animal droppings.

One day Mhepo went to harvest vegetables and left Nemeso playing alone. When she returned, she found Nemeso playing with sand. She heard the sky rumbling and buzzing. She went outside the cave to investigate what was happening and saw a cloud of insects in the atmosphere. Her son continued to play with soil, throwing it in the air. In no time, the insects were making their way into the cave were Nemeso was. The insects made a huge nest near Nemeso. Mhepo was greatly frightened by that occurrence to the extent that she could not fall asleep until the early hours of the morning. In her sleep Mhepo heard a "voice" instructing her to harvest the insects and eat them with her son because they were a relish. The "voice" went on to tell her that the insects were named *harurwa* and that the descendants of Nemeso would all eat these insects. Mhepo was instructed further to clean the insects in warm water and cook them with salt. As we speak these insects are still eaten in Rumedzo and its surrounding areas.

Within a few days, Pfupajena's army began to hunt for Mhepo and her son in the mountain and its surrounding areas. One night Mhepo heard a "voice" instructing her to immediately escape and go raise her child at her parents' home, because Pfupajena's army was fast approaching. When she woke up, she was filled with fear. She looked in all corners of the cave suspecting there was a person inside but did not see anyone. At the break of dawn, Mhepo gathered all her belongings and left and began the journey to her maiden home. It was a taxing journey especially for a woman, but she could do nothing about it because this is what she had been instructed to do by ancestral spirits. She walked hurriedly fearing that Pfupajena's army would catch her. She became relaxed after crossing Save River, because she was confident nobody was following her. Besides, she was now in a territory that fell under the jurisdiction of Chief Mutema, making it difficult for Pfupajena's army to come and attack or capture her.

Chapter Nine

The return of Nemeso

After arriving in her place of birth, Mhepo had to follow laid down traditional procedures. The fact that she was running away from her husband's home without his consent meant she was not supposed to go straight to her parents' home. She approached chief Mutema's senior adviser so he could convey her message to the chief. She told the chief's adviser who she was and where she had come from.

When the chief heard Mhepo's story and saw the strange baby Nemeso with four eyes, he decided to hurriedly make a decision. The chief told his adviser that the issue needed more time to digest, and that it needed deliberation by many people. He likened Mhepo's story to the process of dressing an animal's head. The chief asked his adviser to call other advisers for a meeting the following day.

After the arrival of the chief's advisers, Mhepo's issue was discussed, and the baby Nemeso was brought for everyone present to witness the strange baby. The issue was debated with some saying it would be a curse to have the baby in their area. Others said it was unfair to ask Mhepo to go back to her husband as this could bring about huge misfortunes because of denying a disabled person a place to stay. In those days a person would only be denied residence on the grounds of witchcraft. A witch had one ear cut as a way of warning others of the presence of danger. It was an offence to deny someone who was not a witch a place of residence to the extent that the person denying someone residence would end up being punished by the avenging spirit. There was an avenging spirit called *gandanzara*. If a tramp came to your home and asked for food you were supposed to give them; failure to do so meant your whole family would perish as a result of the tramp's revenge. It was agreed that Mhepo was welcome to stay in chief Mutema's area. Some of the advisers of the chief were asked to build her a home on top of a nearby hill which was near chief Musikavanhu's area of jurisdiction.

Mhepo and her son went to live on the hill where a shelter had been prepared for them. Chief Mutema and Nemeso's grandfather, Musikavanhu, visited Mhepo and her son regularly. One day chief Mutema instructed one of his advisers to kill a fat sheep and give it to Mhepo as a present. Nemeso had become a small boy. When Nemeso saw the chief and his adviser bringing them a sheep, he was very happy. He was so happy that he began to throw sand into the air, creating a scene reminiscent of a place where bulls are fighting. The dust at the scene resembled rain clouds. When the dust subsided, they all heard the hill reverberate with the sound of *harurwa*. After a short time, they saw swarms and swarms of *harurwa* settling near Mhepo. The chief and his adviser were surprised by this occurrence. Chief Mutema looked at Mhepo and realised she was very composed. The chief asked Mhepo the significance of this occurrence. Mhepo gave the chief some of the *harurwa* which she said was a relish. The chief and his adviser were very happy about it. Nemeso became very famous in chief Mutema's area. Even today chief Mutema's area is home to a lot of *harurwa* although the people in that area do not know how to tender them the way it's done in Nerumedzo.

44

Since that occurrence, chief Mutema and his people respected Mhepo and Nemeso. Nemeso was regarded as a spirit medium. He lived with his mother until he was a grown up boy. Although it had been agreed at a meeting by the chief and his advisers that Nemeso was not supposed to be paraded to the people, his fame had grown in leaps and bounds because of his association with *harurwa*. Nemeso became even more famous than chief Mutema himself as people came from all directions just to see how he was. If it was nowadays, he could have earned a lot of money and treasury from tourists from abroad. Even children knew there was this person named Nemeso.

When Nemeso become an adult, his grandfather and uncles held a meeting about what they should do for Nemeso. It was agreed to take Nemeso to his father Pfupajena. Chief Musikavanhu sent word to chief Mutema about their intention, and he was very happy about it. Chief Mutema urged Musikavanhu not to go but to send his advisers. Mutema also seconded his own advisers to accompany Nemeso. These were men of valour and great strength.

Spears, axes, bows and arrows and knives were sharpened in preparation for the journey to the land of the Duma because the forests were infested with dangerous predators. There was also suspicion that they might face hostilities because of the way Mhepo and Nemeso left the land of the Duma. They did not spend many days to get to chief Pfupajena's area, because they were walking both during the day and at night. They rested when they arrived in headman Chigumisirwa's area named Beta. This is where they built their temporary shelter and then sent a message to chief Pfupajena about the purpose of their visit. Nemeso remained guarded by some very strong men, because they feared he might be attacked from any and all directions. What surprised the people who had been assigned to guard Nemeso was the ease with which they killed animals for food.

The messengers assigned to tell chief Pfupajena about the return of Nemeso were six men led by Manenga, the great warrior and spirit medium. They woke up early in the morning and walked towards Pfupajena's home. They arrived at the chief's court at the break of day. They found two of Pfupajena's advisers who also wanted to meet the chief. These advisers were known as Gwekwe and Mandiki. The advance party sent to Pfupajena did the traditional greeting rituals and then sat on stones surrounding the fire where Gwekwe and Mandiki were warming themselves. They exchanged a few pleasantries. Manenga and his delegation engaged Gwekwe and Mandiki in conversation. Manenga was the most senior of the people who had accompanied Nemeso. He carried his bows and arrows. Manenga had bloodshot eyes. He was very tall and muscular. Manenga's physique was intimidating to anyone who met him especially those who did not know his personality. Manenga introduced his team and revealed that they had been sent by Musikavanhu and wanted to see chief Pfupajena. Pfupajena's chief adviser immediately arrived at the chief's court. His duties included awakening the chief before anyone else arrived at the chief's court. On this particular day, he had been late and so did not wait to get to know the people already present. When he got to the chief's bedroom, he did all the greeting formalities with the chief.

After greeting the chief, the senior adviser took his walking stick and knobkerrie and went back to the fireplace where the guests of Musikavanhu waited. The chief emerged holding a container of water and ash to clean his teeth. After doing so, he returned to his bedroom to wear leopard skin and a headdress. He took a container with snuff and his knobkerrie and went out. The chief's principal adviser did not sit down because he knew the chief was about to arrive. When the chief arrived, those present at his fireplace all did the formal rituals of greeting, and the chief promptly sat down on his beautifully curved chair.

The chief's senior adviser led in the rituals performed at the chief's fireplace. This particular day was billed for discussions on rain petitioning ceremonies. That was the purpose of Gwekwe and Mandiki's visit. They wanted to discuss with the chief about preparations for this day. It was resolved that the visitors from Musikavanhu would be attended to first. Long ago, visitors from afar were respected and always accorded the first opportunity on such occasions. Pfupajena acknowledged the presence of his visitors and asked Gweke to tell him who the visitors were and the purpose of their visit. Gwekwe told the chief that the visitors had been sent by Musikavanhu. He then asked the visitors themselves to formally tell the chief who they were and the purpose of their visit.

The visitors disclosed that they had been sent by both chiefs Musikavanhu and Mutema. Pfupajena was surprised but went on to ask the visitors to continue their story. The spokesman for the visitors went ahead and said they had come to tell him that his child Nemeso who had been condemned to death was still alive and was not dead as the chief would have preferred. The chief was frightened by this disclosure. The chief asked about the whereabouts of Nemeso. He went on to say that according to their tradition, a deformed baby should be killed, and he was not sure what

47

could be done because Nemeso was now a grown up. Pfupajena asked where Nemeso was so that he could send his people to see him but went on to say that he did not want to see Nemeso himself as he feared that he would die.

Manenga answered back by saying that the child was Pfupajena's and queried how long the chief wanted Nemeso to live with his uncles rather than his own people. He added that part of his mission was to hear from Pfupajena how long Musikavanhu should look after Nemeso, while he had a father. Manenga revealed to the chief that they had left Nemeso in the mountains to the east so as to seek permission to bring Nemeso to the chief's court.

Chief Pfupajena answered that he was offering Nemeso the area to the east. Nemeso would rule that area, and no one else would be allowed to have control over it. Pfupajena also offered Manenga and the other members of his delegation an area where they could come and live as a way of thanking them for having looked after Nemeso. Even today this area is ruled by people of the Beta totem of chief Musikavanhu under headman Nebeta.

Chapter Ten

The reign and magical powers of Nemeso

As time progressed, Pfupajena began to ponder about Nemeso. He decided to call his uncle Mutindi and some of his advisers to a meeting to discuss issues having to do with Nemeso. After deliberating on this issue, it was agreed that Mutindi who is the great ancestor of the Mukanganwi chieftainship would demarcate the area to be occupied by Musikavanhu's messengers and the area to the east to be occupied by Nemeso near the Mambiru mountains.

Arrangements for the journey to visit Nemeso got underway. Chief Pfupajena educated Mutindi and his advisers about important information pertaining to the Pfupajena chieftaincy. He told the delegation that they should tell Nemeso that they would remain sworn enemies to eternity. The chief went on to say that Nemeso would reside in the hilly area he named Rumedzo. Nemeso was going to be the supreme leader of the area. Pfupajena disclosed that he would never visit the area under the rule of Nemeso, and that he would never cross rivers of the area nor drink water in that area, and this up to the end of Pfupajena's dynasty.

After this briefing by Pfupajena, Mutindi and the chief's advisers began their journey to the east where Nemeso had remained. They did everything as instructed by Pfupajena. After this, they toured the Rumedzo area including the Mambiru mountain where Nemeso was raised. They went into the cave where Nemeso and Mhepo had lived. They climbed to the summit of Mambiru and saw how large an area Rumedzo was, how beautiful it was and how amply

49

endowed it was with forests and rivers flowing down to all directions. They saw the sources of rivers like Gande, Mukore, Mujiche, Musaizi, Madowaire, Surudzurwi, Chivaka, and Chiyenge. After this, they blew a horn which was heard everywhere including in Pfupajena's court.

After Pfupajena's advisers and messengers had left, Nemeso went to live in the cave in which he had been raised by his mother. They relished mainly *harurwa* during those years. Nemeso was assisted by his uncles and the messengers of his grandfather Musikavanhu who had brought him to Duma. They had come to live in the area allocated to them by Pfupajena.

Meanwhile, some of Pfupajena's advisers heard that Nemeso, who was supposed to be killed because he was a curse, born deformed, had been allocated huge tracts of land through the orders of his father Pfupajena. They became jealous. With knives sharpened, they plotted against Nemeso. They planned to kill Nemeso by organizing a war to take the land that had been allocated to him. They hatched a plan, that of surrounding Mambiru mountain and hunting for Nemeso and his guards. They would then kill Nemeso and his aids.

A crack regiment known as *Dzviti ramambo* (the king's ruthless army) was put on alert by the chief's senior advisers. Spears and knives were sharpened in preparation for war. The fighters headed towards Rumedzo to fight Nemeso regain land under his jurisdiction.

At Rumedzo, Nemeso lived with Manenga, the head of delegation when Nemeso was brought from Musikavanhu's area. Manenga was a famed and highly regarded warrior in chief Mutema's chiefdom. He was particularly famous for his wizardry in the use of a bow and arrows. He was a marksman of repute.This earned him the nickname "Haripotse" (One who do not miss). When fighting he would become possessed and would almost single-handedly destroy the enemy.

On the eve of the attack by *Dzviti ramambo*, Nemeso could not fall asleep and told Manenga he was going to sleep outside the cave. Nemeso took his *gudza* (blanket) and went outside the cave. He went and slept on a rock. After falling asleep, he dreamt of a lion approaching him. The lion turned into a human being and warned him that he was about to be attacked. Nemeso was, however, reassured that he would be protected. On waking up, Nemeso rushed to the cave to alert Manenga. Manenga said that this must be true, because such a message had also been communicated to him by his medium. The two alerted their fighters to prepare for imminent war.

Before the break of dawn, Nemeso's soldiers had surrounded the mountain waiting in ambush. Manenga had blown his kudu horn. He kept two kudu horns, one was big and the other small. When he blew the smaller horn, it meant there was peace, but if he blew the bigger one, it meant there was an impending war. His bigger horn was mainly to alert the people about an impending Ndebele raid, as during those years the latter could come anytime. The Ndebele mainly raided for grain, cattle and beautiful women.

When the sun rose, Nemeso and his people saw a large army headed in their direction. Dust rose up around the invaders, who divided themselves into two groups as they surrounded the mountain. They were singing their war song.

Leader: *Gwindingwi shumba inoruma*

Chorus: *Awoyewoye inoruma*

L: *Vana vaPfupajena vachauya, hezvo machinda mose muchachema. Gwindingwi ishumba inoruma*

C: *Gwindingwi ishumba inoruma*

L: *Awoyewoye inoruma*

C: *Vana vaPfupajena vachauya, hezvo machinda mose muchachema. Ggwindingwi ishumba inoruma*

L: *Gwindingwi ishumba inoruma*

C: *Awoyewoye inoruma*

L: *Vana vaPfupajena vachauya, hezvo machinda mose muchachema. Ggwindingwi ishumba inoruma*

Nemeso's fighters, upon hearing this war song by the *Dzviti ramambo*, put boulders in place. Led by Nemeso and Manenga, they also broke into their war song. Baboons and monkeys emerged from caves and fled in all directions. Nemeso and his army sang their war song so powerfully that the root of the mountain shook.

Leader: *Nyuchi dzinoruma!*

Chorus: *Tora uta hwangu ndoda kuenda dzinoruma*

L: *Mhandu VaShewoye*

C: *He-e dzinoruma*

L: *Nhandi VaManenga!*

C: *Torai uta hwenyu toda kuenda dzinoruma*

L: *Nyuchi dzinoruma*

C: *He-e dzinoruma*

L: *Mhandu VaShewoye*

C: *He-e dzinoruma*

L: *Nhandi VaManenga!*

C: *Torai uta hwenyu toda kuenda dzinoruma*

Leading his army in war was an easy task for Nemeso, because he could see with his two eyes in front and the other two at the back. The *Dzviti* regiment ascended the mountain, and Nemeso and his soldiers let go huge boulders towards the enemy positions. The boulders crashed the *Dzviti ramambo* soldiers creating mayhem at the foot of the mountain. Some tried to hide behind trees but boulders came down crushing both the tree and the soldier. Some tried to escape but in vain. Many soldiers of the *Dzviti* regiment died. All of Nemeso's soldiers survived. Nemeso's victory made him a folkhero in chief Pfupajena's area and its environs. The name Rumedzo became well known even beyond the Pfupajena chiefdom.

After his victory, Nemeso moved to a mountain named Nemahwi which is adjacent to a forest where *harurwa* are found. Wherever chief Nemeso lived, *harurwa* would follow him.

Chapter Eleven

Growth of Nemeso's family

After having settled in the Nemahwi mountain, Nemeso got married. His wife fell pregnant and gave birth to a son who was named Nemahwi meaning that they had survived during the battle with the *Dzviti ramambo*, the king's ruthless army. The child was raised and grew into a big boy before Nemeso had another child. It was a common tradition that when a woman was breastfeeding, the mother would not engage in sexual activities. When a man had two or more wives, he would allow his breastfeeding wife time to raise her child and would engage in sexual activities with other wives not breastfeeding. The breastfeeding mother would not get angry with this practice, as it was a common and well respected one. Given that there were no contraceptives such as birth control pills, the mother could fall pregnant while still breast feeding, and the baby would fall ill. Also, women who fell pregnant while breastfeeding would be regarded as women of low morals and become the laughing stock in the whole community.

After the war, Nemeso went back to the cave in the mountain where he was raised. Nemahwi was weaned, and Nemeso's wife fell pregnant and gave birth to a baby boy named Rapfirwa. The message behind that name was that Nemeso was protesting that his father rejected him when he was born. Rapfirwa was Nemeso's last son.

Nemahwi and Rapfirwa grew to become nice young men still living in the Nemahwi mountain to the south *(chamhembe)* of Rumedzo or Mambiru across the Mukore river. Nemahwi by virtue of being the older boy was the first to marry. Nemeso invited his sons to a meeting. Nemeso told Nemahwi that after he married, he should go and settle where he had been born to start his own dynasty. Rapfirwa was told to remain behind in the Rumedzo. Rapfirwa was anointed the heir-apparent to the Nemeso dynasty.

After holding a discussion with his sons, Nemeso feared another attack by Pfupajena and left and started wondering in the forests. He went towards the south (*maodzanyemba*). He settled in the Bvuma mountain in the Matsai area which was under the jurisdiction of chief Neurungwe and shared boundaries with chief Hove's territory.

Nemahwi did as instructed by his father and went and lived in the Nemahwi mountain for which he was named. Nemahwi married, and he was blessed with two sons, Tambara and Mugumisi, who play the role of kingmakers of the Rumedzo dynasty even today.

Rapfirwa also married, and his wife gave birth to six children, some of whom ascended the Rumedzo throne. These children [who ascended the Rumedzo throne] were Chibatya, Machena, Rushambwa, Kuirikira, and Chapwanya, the last born.

After realising that Rumedzo was beautiful and rich in mineral resources, Pfupajena was filled with envy. He decided to renege on what he had promised. Pfupajena had promised Nemeso that Rumedzo would be his and his descendants.

Chapter Twelve

The demise of Nemeso

As typical of Nemeso, he attracted *harurwa* everywhere he stayed. Soon, there were lots of *harurwa* in the Bvuma mountain. Because of this occurrence, Nemeso became very famous in the whole Matsai area. Pfupajena and his sons Gundiro and Mutindi heard about Nemeso. Young Mutindi had been named after his grandfather's young brother, Mutindi, who had assisted in the escape of Mhepo and Nemeso. Age and ill health had caught up with Pfupajena. Mutindi and Gundiro did not visit Nemeso, because they feared his magical powers especially against the background that their father, Pfupajena, had nurtured a perpetual grudge to kill him.

Chief Neurungwe was very happy with the advent of *harurwa* in his drought prone area. Certainly, they would help tremendously to ease the severity of famine and drought in bad years when rain was scarce. Neurungwe was also particularly happy with the idea of Nemeso settling in the Bvuma mountain, because the mountain was the source of a longstanding border dispute between Neurungwe and chief Hove. Neurungwe had heard so much about Nemeso's magical powers and banked on these powers to vanquish Hove in the event that the latter waged a war against him. As a gesture of his gratitude to Nemeso, Neurungwe made available to Nemeso a team of mbira players who would entertain Nemeso who was now advanced in age.

One day, Hove decided to launch an attack on Neurungwe so as to take over Bvuma mountain and its surrounding areas. Hove's army was comprised of very strong men. Neurungwe immediately made a passionate appeal for help from Nemeso. He was at pains in telling Nemeso that he was not prepared for war and that Hove's soldiers outnumbered his. Nemeso sympathized with Neurungwe and told him to go back, while Nemeso immediately fell asleep.While asleep, he saw a vision of the same lion he had seen in his dream while residing in Mambiru. The lion came closer to him and told him to reciprocate the hospitality he had been accorded by Neurungwe. Nemeso was instructed to help Neurungwe by using the same method he used while in Mambiru.When he woke up, he saw Neurungwe approaching him. Some of Nemeso's eyes were still closed, so Neurungwe did not want to bother him. He sat on a rock near Nemeso. Neurungwe was still shaken by the impending war with Hove.

After a while, Nemeso rose up and walked towards Neurungwe. He began to tell Neurungwe that he had nothing to fear and asked that his soldiers come to Bvuma mountain. Nemeso promised that he would lead these soldiers in battle and that there would be no casualties on his side. Neurungwe immediately left and organised his army as instructed by Nemeso. Neurungwe asked his senior adviser to blow the war trumpet and to assemble all fighters quickly. The soldiers were told to climb Bvuma mountain and adequately prepare for war against Hove. Spears, bows and arrows, knives and axes were all sharpened in preparation for war. The soldiers then went up Bvuma mountain, and all bowed before Nemeso as had been instructed by the chief. This was a sign of great respect by Neurungwe and his army to Nemeso. Nemeso instructed Neurungwe's soldiers each to stand next to a boulder. Nemeso would then blow his trumpet, and the soldiers would release the boulders.

On the other side, Hove's soldiers were bubbling with confidence. They thought that because they outnumbered their enemy they would easily overwhelm Neurungwe's army. Moreover, they knew that their chief, Hove, had not given Neurungwe adequate notice of their intention to fight him. They did not know that Neurungwe had done his homework by enlisting the services of Nemeso.

The following day, Hove's army went to Bvuma because they had heard that Neurungwe's soldiers were hiding there. They broke into song to boost their morale and frighten their enemy. They sang as follows:

Leader: *Mbavarira inoda vane dare*
Chorus: *Hoyehoye!*
L: *Vashevangu*
C: *Iyawoye yowerere!*
L: *Chinezengwe akafira pabani apo*
C: *Hoye hoye!*
L: *Vashe hoye*
C: *Iyawoye yowerere!*
L: *Mbavarira inoda vane dare*
C: *Hoye hoye!*
L: *Vashe hoye*
C: *Iyawoye yowerere!*
L: *Chinezengwe akafira pabani apo*
C: *Hoye hoye!*
L: *Vashe hoye*
C: *Hoye hoye!*

After the sun had risen, Hove's army arrived at Bvuma Mountain. The deep voices of Hove's soldiers resonated throughout the area as they sang their war song threatening to devour their enemy. Because Hove's soldiers were many, they decided to surround the whole mountain so that not even a single enemy soldier would escape. When they began climbing the mountain, Nemeso blew his trumpet to signal Neurungwe's soldiers to release the boulders. There was pandemonium in the Hove camp. Howling and wailing filled the air as boulders rolled down the mountain crushing Hove's soldiers. Not many of them managed to escape. The few who survived were badly injured. Neurungwe was victorious because of Nemeso's military genius. Nemeso's fame spread, because people knew it was he who had masterminded this victory.

Hove was not amused that he lost the war. He vented his anger on Nemeso who had assisted Neurungwe with daring strategies that marked the end of many of his gallant soldiers. Hove knew that if he was to fight Neurungwe and defeat him, he first had to deal with Nemeso. He hatched a plan to kill Nemeso first before he would revenge his defeat to Neurungwe. He knew there were mbira players who entertained Nemeso. He decided to bribe the mbira players especially the lead mbira player.

After Hove realised that his relationship with the mbira players had become strong, he told them about his plan to kill Nemeso. It was known that when Nemeso was asleep, two of his eyes would be closed and the other two would be open seeing all that was happening. The idea was to play the mbira until all his four eyes closed. Hove promised to reward the would-be assassins with many cattle, women and pieces of land.

The mbira players easily agreed to this plan. Moreover they were not happy with the remuneration they were receiving from Neurungwe. The mbira players performed as they had never performed before. Nemeso fell asleep and closed two of his eyes, and within a short time the other two closed as well. This was the golden opportunity to strike. Hove had bribed Gambure to kill Nemeso as soon as he fell asleep. Gambure did not waste time and immediately stabbed Nemeso in the neck and fled away without removing the spear. Gambure knew that if Neurungwe discovered he had killed Nemeso, he would be sentenced to death.This was what was practiced long ago – you kill and you get killed as well. This is captured in the proverb that those who live by the sword die by the sword.

When chief Hove heard the news of Nemeso's death, he launched another attack on Neurungwe the following day. Neurungwe was taken by surprise, as he was in the process of mourning Nemeso. Hove's soldiers burnt Neurungwe's homes and killed all men they met along the way. They captured women, children and cattle. Neurungwe and some of his advisers hid in a cave in the Bvuma Mountain and came out at night and ran away. Some of Hove's soldiers did not immediately go back, because they realised that Neurungwe had escaped. They guarded Nemeso's corpse suspecting that some people would attempt to bury the corpse because Nemeso was very much respected by Neurungwe and his people.

When Neurungwe heard about the death of Nemeso, he was very troubled. He sent eight men to collect Nemeso's body to give it a decent burial in a cave to the south (*maodzanyemba*) of Bvuma Mountain. They did not know that some of Hove's soldiers were waiting in ambush. Neurungwe's men took the body and walked towards the place where they had been instructed to bury Nemeso. Hove's soldiers who had been hiding attacked Neurungwe's men such that the latter only managed to put Nemeso's body in between two rock boulders and ran away.

-End-